Creative Crafts for Creative Hands

DRIED & PRESSED
FLOWERS

© Eaglemoss Publications Ltd. 1990, 1991, 1992, 1993
All rights reserved

CLB 4125
This edition published in 1995 by Tiger Books International PLC, London
© 1995 CLB Publishing, Godalming, Surrey
Printed and bound in Proost, N.V. Belgium
All rights reserved
ISBN 1-85501-592-7

Managing Editor: Jo Finnis
Editors: Sue Wilkinson; Geraldine Christy
Jacket and prelim design: Art of Design
Typesetting: Litho Link Ltd, Welshpool, Powys
Production: Ruth Arthur; Sally Connolly; Neil Randles; Karen Staff; Jonathan Tickner;
Matthew Dale
Director of Production: Gerald Hughes

Photographers
Jacket John Suett/Eaglemoss; Jacket flap Steve Tanner/Eaglemoss; Title page Graham
Rae/Eaglemoss; 9 Insight Picture Library; 10 (t) Sue Atkinson/Eaglemoss; 10 (b) Steve
Tanner/Eaglemoss; 11 Steve Tanner/Eaglemoss; 12 Steve Tanner/Eaglemoss; 13 Elizabeth
Whiting Associates; 14 Elizabeth Whiting Associates; 15 (tl) Insight Picture Library; 15
(r) John Suett/Eaglemoss; 15 (b) John Suett/Eaglemoss; 16 Elizabeth Whiting Associates;
17-19 John Suett/Eaglemoss; 21 Elizabeth Whiting Associates; 22 Simon Page-
Ritchie/Eaglemoss; 23-25 Steve Tanner/Eaglemoss; 26 (tl) Elizabeth Whiting Associates;
26 (tr) Robert Harding Picture Library; 26 (b) Maison Marie Claire; 27 Elizabeth Whiting
Associates; 28 (t) Garden Picture Library; 28 (bl) Garden Picture Library; 28 (br) Insight
Picture Library; 29-32 John Suett/Eaglemoss; 33 Ariadne Holland; 35 Araidne Holland;
36 Elizabeth Whiting Associates; 37-38 Graham Rae/Eaglemoss 39 Insight Picture
Library; 40 Martin Norris/Eaglemoss; 41 Elizabeth Whiting Associates; 42 Steve
Tanner/Eaglemoss; 43 Jon Bouchier;44 John Suett/Eaglemoss; 45-48 Elizabeth Whiting
Associates; 49 Steve Tanner/Eaglemoss; 52 Steve Tanner/Eaglemoss; 53-56 Sue
Atkinson/Eaglemoss; 57-58 Steve Tanner/Eaglemoss; 59 John Suett/Eaglemoss

Illustrators
20 Jenny Abbott/Garden Studio; 22 Michael Shoebridge; 34-35 Michael Shoebridge; 38
Terry Evans; 44 Michael Shoebridge; 38 Terry Evans; 44 Michael Shoebridge; 47-48
Elisabeth Dowle; 50-52 Liz Pepperell/Garden Studio; 55 Michael Shoebridge; 58
Elisabeth Dowle; 60 John Hutchinson

Creative Crafts for Creative Hands

DRIED & PRESSED
FLOWERS

*How to make beautiful gifts and objects for the home,
from basic techniques to finishing touches.*

**TIGER BOOKS INTERNATIONAL
LONDON**

Contents

Flowers forever

The exciting variety of dried flowers and grasses now available makes it possible to have permanent floral arrangements as lovely as any fresh flower display.

Dried flowers can be arranged to complement your surroundings, or to remind you of particular landscapes. Their subtle, natural colours bring a touch of summer to winter, the countryside to the city.

Selecting plants and colours

With just two or three bunches of different types of dried flowers from a flower shop, you can enjoy making an appealing display. It's hard to go wrong with dried flowers, especially now that the too vivid colours of artificially dyed flowers are a thing of the past.

Before facing the bewildering variety of flowers for sale, it's worth thinking about colours and shapes. First, think of colour combinations that particularly appeal to you, and which may already be in evidence in your home. If you like yellow and orange, or blue and pink, you can choose dried flowers in those colours, with perhaps one bunch in a more neutral colour, such as cream, to provide background.

Alternatively, stick to shades of one colour and plan your display around that theme. It's also a good idea to allow for a variety of shapes and textures, balancing seedheads, twigs and grasses with flowers.

Containers

There are no hard and fast rules about how to arrange dried flowers, or about where to put them. For an immediately charming and rustic effect, you can make simple bouquets and hang them on the wall or against cupboard doors.

Alternatively, use some of the ready-made containers lying about your home such as old jugs, bowls and teapots. Dried flowers don't need watering, so the containers don't need to be waterproof. Wooden boxes and baskets are often favoured because of their natural colours, which tone so well with the muted colours of naturally dried flowers. Waste paper baskets, bicycle baskets and sewing baskets will also do nicely. Smaller baskets, boxes and pots need to be weighted, with pebbles perhaps, so that they don't become top heavy when you put flowers in them.

▲ **Floral colour**
Natural and dyed seedheads, everlasting flowers and bold orange Chinese lanterns are just some of the dried flowers that are available for displays. Large department stores, florists and gift shops have a selection for you to choose from.

A flower basket for all seasons

Six different dried flowers nestle in a dark rustic basket to provide a colourful and lasting decoration to any hallway or living room.

Materials
Sea lavender (*Limonium latifolium*)
Pink everlasting flowers (*Helichrysum bracteatum*)
Yarrow (*Achillea filipendulina*)
Purple and pink statice (*Limonium sinuatum*)
Love-in-a-mist (*Nigella damascena*)
Sea holly (*Eryngium*)
Apart from the flowers, you need scissors, a craft knife, florist's foam, three to four handfuls of sphagnum moss and some stub wire pins.

Yarrow

Sea holly

purple and pink statice

ARRANGING THE FLOWERS

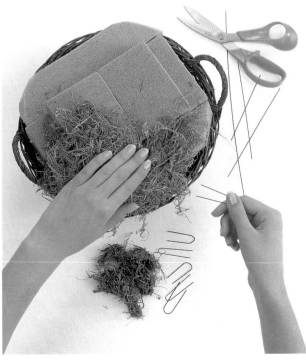

1 Prepare the base Cut the foam to fit your basket, putting any leftover sections on top to make a domed shape. Take the sphagnum moss and pin it all over the foam, using medium wire bent like a hairpin.

Love-in-a-mist

Sea lavender

pink everlasting flowers

2 Arranging the background Cut the sea lavender into sections 15-20cm (6-8in) long and make a basic dome shape. In your mind, divide the shape into quarters and, using sprigs of wired yellow yarrow, highlight each one with the same number of flowerheads.

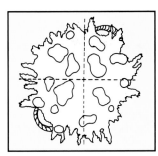

3 Purple statice Separate the bunch of purple statice into sprigs and gently insert them into your arrangement. Turn the basket as you work so that you get a round, even shape as defined by the sea lavender.

4 Pink statice Add sprigs of pink statice, working across the basket in a zigzag, from the front to the back. This helps to achieve a more abstract impression of overall colour. The pink flowers should not be in circles.

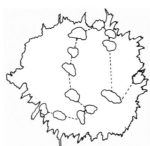
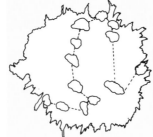

5 Adding bunches Wire together small bunches of sea holly and love-in-a-mist seed pods. Take each of the bunches and insert them at random.

tip

Additional support
Many dried flowers, yarrow, for example, have brittle stems. With the help of artificial wire stems, they can be used more easily. Take a length of stub wire and bend one end to form a small hook. Feed the straight end through the centre of the flowerhead until the hook catches firmly, out of sight, in the middle of the bloom.

To wire a sprig place a length of stub wire through the sprig, then bend both ends down and secure by twisting round the stalk. To wire a spray, gather four or five flowers or seedheads together and bind with a length of stub wire.

6 Final touches Take the pink everlasting flowers, wire any weak stems or broken heads, then add them to the arrangement. Start at the top, inserting the flowers to form a small crown, then work downwards, turning the basket regularly.

Drying flowers

Massed in baskets glowing with glorious reds, golds, faded pinks and purples, plaited into delicate wedding garlands, or arranged in tiny individual table decorations, dried flowers from your own garden are a delight. Although there is probably nothing to beat the charm of a huge bowl of fresh roses or sweet peas, dried flowers have a real beauty of their own, and of course, a permanence unmatched by theire fresh counterparts. With dried flowers you can choose colour schemes and textures to suit any mood or decorative theme. The possibilities you can achieve are limited only by your time and your imagination.

Buying dried flowers can be very expensive, especially if you want generous quantities to fill a simple basket or two. So drying your own flowers and foliage can be rewarding in both a creative and an economic sense.

Growing and gathering your own
For gardeners who are also dried flower enthusiasts, nurserymen are producing lots of ideal plants: favourites include Bells of Ireland, Chinese lanterns, clary sage, scabious, love-in-a-mist, strawflowers, immortelles, statice, zinnia, achillea and honesty, but with a little trial and error you will find that you can successfully dry all kinds of garden flowers and foliage.

As the grower you will have the huge advantage of being able to capture and preserve your favourites at their most perfect. You can also use hedgerow and woodland material, but be very careful not to touch any protected species, and never uproot any plant from the wild.

Always choose a dry sunny day for picking. Wait until the dew dries off the flowers, but don't linger until the flowers begin to wilt in the heat. For perfect

▲ Silver, gold and cream
There are no very unusual plants in this arrangement of air-dried flowers and grasses, but the combination of silvery whites, creams and golds gives this basket great visual impact. Among its ingredients are honesty, molucella, gypsophila, helichrysum and carline thistles.

blooms, pick only those that are just about to open, when they are at their peak of colour and condition. Plants with tassels and catkins should be picked when immature, before the pollen drops; pick seedpods as soon as the petals fall, or the seed will fall out as the plant dries. If you are buying from a florist, explain that you are going to dry the flowers and take advice on the best blooms to choose.

The two easiest ways to preserve plants are air drying and pressing; pre-

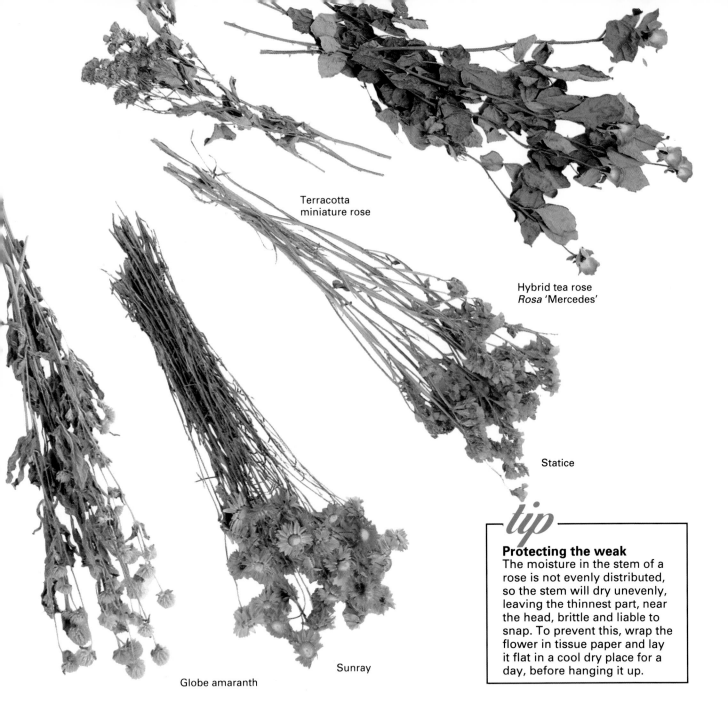

Terracotta
miniature rose

Hybrid tea rose
Rosa 'Mercedes'

Statice

Globe amaranth

Sunray

tip

Protecting the weak
The moisture in the stem of a rose is not evenly distributed, so the stem will dry unevenly, leaving the thinnest part, near the head, brittle and liable to snap. To prevent this, wrap the flower in tissue paper and lay it flat in a cool dry place for a day, before hanging it up.

serving with glycerine and chemical drying is described on pages 17–20.

Air drying

Drying plants in the air is the simplest method of all, requiring no special equipment or techniques and it is suitable for a very large number of plants. Air drying can be done in three ways: standing, hanging or lying flat.

Standing flowers

Pampas grass, sea lavender, statice, astilbe, spiraea and Chinese lanterns all dry beautifully simply standing in empty vases in dry, well-aired positions. Many foliage plants, such as ferns and bracken dry well in this way.

Fully mature hydrangeas, Bells of Ireland, proteas and heathers keep their colour better if you start the drying process by standing them in 5cm (2in) of cold water. Keep the vase in a warm room, so that the plants dry as quickly as possible. When all the liquid has been absorbed, allow the plants to continue the drying process naturally.

Flowers with wide or fragile heads, such as fennel or giant allium, should be dried standing upright, supported in florist's foam or chicken wire.

Hanging flowers

Larkspur, roses, poppy heads, gypsophila, lady's mantle and achillea and many grasses respond well to being hung. Large flowers should be hung up individually, but small flowers can be hung in bunches. You should restrict the bunches to one type of flower only, as drying times vary for each plant.

To hang bunches of flowers, first remove most of the foliage, and any thorns, and bind the stems together with rubber bands or wire. You can use string or raffia for a more natural look, but rubber bands have the advantage of contracting as the stems shrink so the bunch doesn't start to disintegrate, and wires can be easily tightened. Keep the bunches small and the flowerheads apart to prevent rot and crushing.

Air should be able to circulate freely around the bunches, which can be hung from hooks on ceilings or walls, or from clothes racks, hangers or bamboo canes fixed across the ceiling. It is important that the air should be cool (but not less than 10°C, 50°F) and dry, perhaps in a little-used room or attic; kitchens and garden sheds tend to be damp and are not ideal. The flowers should be dried out of the sunlight in order to preserve their colours.

Some plants, such as strawflowers, have very brittle stems when they are dry. To prevent the heads snapping off while you are arranging them, wire them first (see page 12).

WIRING A ROSE

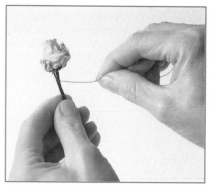

1 Hold the flower head gently in one hand and snip off the stem about 5cm (2in) from the head. Attach a medium stub wire to the remaining stem with reel wire.

2 Starting just below the flower head, wind green or brown gutta-percha tape around the whole length of the extended stem.

▲ **Air drying at home**
Air drying flowers is very easy, and even if you don't want to arrange them immediately, the dried bunches can be stored most attractively.

Drying flat

Grasses and plants with delicate or fragile stems should be dried flat. Lay the plants in a single layer on several sheets of newspaper or cardboard and keep in a dry place. The plants should be turned over at intervals to ensure even drying. Dry lavender in this way.

Pressing

Pressing is as simple as air drying with the difference that plant material preserved in this way will retain its colour. (see pages 50–51).

Simply lay leaves such as fern, beech and oak between layers of newspaper and place under a carpet.

▲ **Air drying – hanging method**
Join small bunches of one type of flower together with rubber bands and hang upside down.

◄ **Air drying – standing method**
Some flowers, such as echinops and hydrangea, should be stood in a little water and left to dry.

15

▼ **Hanging baskets**
*A simple arrangement of air-dried flowers and grasses –
helichrysums, yarrow, poppy heads and barley – look
dramatic hanging against a white-washed wall.*

▲ **A flowery touch**
*A bunch of dried flowers, including immortelles,
anaphalis, alchemilla, zinnias, lavender and gypsophila
gives a delightfully informal finishing touch to a lacy
window blind.*

tip

**Microwaved
flowers**
This method has
proved successful for
reducing the air drying
process for roses,
gypsophila and
grasses from two or
three weeks to two or
three days.
Method Strip leaves
and lay flowers on
several sheets of
kitchen paper. At 400-
500 watts, cook for 2½
minutes (roses) or 3
minutes (gypsophila).

▶ **A many splendoured thing**
*Dried flowers are not always muted
in colour – this vibrant arrangement
contains artemisia, larkspur,
hydrangea, poppy heads,
strawflowers with silica dried roses
and glycerined eucalyptus.*

Preserving flowers

The commonest way to preserve flowers and plants is air drying – by hanging in bunches, standing in vases, or pressing between several layers of newspaper.

However, some flowers are too delicate to respond well to this treatment, and require a more elaborate method of preserving – desiccation or drying in chemicals or sand. This method is very ancient – apparently the Egyptians dried garlands of flowers in sand for the dead to take with them to the underworld, and this method of flower preservation has flourished ever since.

Flowers dried in this way are terribly delicate and the method is quite fiddly, expensive, and not always successful, but to repay all the effort the results can be stunning, with blooms that look as fragile and perfect as their fresh counterparts. Daffodils, primroses, camellias and orchids respond beautifully to chemical desiccation and it could be the perfect way to preserve some blooms from a special occasion – a wedding, anniversary or birthday.

Glycerine or antifreeze

Dried tree and shrub branches are essential to provide the necessary foliage for large arrangements, and are generally very difficult to buy, so it's important to be able to create your own. Foliage preserved in glycerine or antifreeze is very supple, can be washed or wiped clean, lasts indefinitely and can be successfully combined with fresh, dried or artificial flowers.

Foliage for treating with glycerine or antifreeze is easy to come by; tree material can be gathered from the wild without damage – beech, oak, horse chestnut, hazel, birch, holly and ivy. Even the smallest, shadiest garden can usually produce the odd shrub, and you will find that careful light pruning in your own and your friends' gardens will produce plenty of shrubby material without making ugly gaps in the borders. Amongst suitable common shrubs are box, ivy, magnolia, mahonia, laurel, fatsia, cotoneaster and eucalyptus.

◀ **All season arrangement**
This unusual hall table arrangement combines foliage from the garden – ivy and laurel – and dramatic orange- veined leaves from a croton, all of which have been preserved in glycerine, with fir cones and twisted twigs.

tip

Artificial colour
Some green leaves, when treated with glycerine, may turn a muddy khaki, and ivy can turn an unattractive yellow: try adding a few drops of green food colouring to counteract this effect.

Materials
For preserving in glycerine:
Glycerine or **antifreeze**
For desiccating:
Silica gel crystals or **borax** and **silver sand** or **alum** and **silver sand**
Large airtight container
Chicken wire
Sieve
Slotted spoon

The best time of year to gather foliage for preserving is late summer, when the branches and leaves are mature but not too old. Don't wait until autumn to pick deciduous material, because the leaves will have stopped absorbing sap, and will not absorb glycerine either; evergreens are also at their best at this time of year.

Plant material preserved in this way retains the strength and suppleness of the original plant, which makes it easy to arrange, but you will find that the method causes dramatic changes in the colour of the foliage. For instance, eucalyptus leaves dried in the air will be brittle and silvery-grey, whereas glycerined eucalyptus will be supple but a rich tawny brown in colour. Leaves with a naturally brown tint will turn a rich dark or bronzy hue.

Some flowers also respond well to glycerine treatment, for instance molucella and hydrangea, but the method works best on foliage.

PRESERVING FOLIAGE IN GLYCERINE

1 Preparing the foliage First remove the lower leaves, and make sharp angled cuts so that the plant absorbs the glycerine solution. With heavy woody stems you should crush the ends to help absorption.

2 Using the preserving fluid Soak the stems in water for a couple of hours, and then plunge them into preserving solution made from either 40% glycerine and 60% boiling water, or a 50-50 solution of antifreeze and boiling water. The plants should be supported in deep, narrow containers in between 7.5-10cm (3-4in) of the solution, and kept in a dark place.

3 Completing the process Top up the solution frequently until the foliage feels smooth and the leaves have completely changed colour.

Individual leaves and sprigs can be treated by floating them in a glycerine or antifreeze/water solution until their colour changes. Remove and wash them in a mild detergent and then lay them flat on sheets of newspaper to dry.

Drying with desiccants

This method is best suited to large flowers like lilies, daffodils and roses. Blooms preserved in this way look very like the original fresh flowers, but they are very fragile and sensitive to moisture in the atmosphere.

Various desiccants can be used, but the commonest are silica gel crystals, silver sand, borax and alum. Silica gel crystals, which you can buy from some chemists, photographic shops or from florists' suppliers, may be very coarse. Break down the crystals with a rolling pin until they resemble caster sugar.

Borax and alum are both used with silver sand; the mixture is three parts of either borax or alum to two parts silver sand. These work in the same way as silica crystals in removing all moisture from the flowers, but they take rather longer to work: silica-dried flowers take between 2-6 days, sand-dried between 7-10 days.

Storing dried flowers

If you are not going to use your dried flowers immediately, store them in a cool, dry place, either hanging in bunches, or laid in boxes, with their heads protected in layers of tissue.

▶ **Silica dried anemones**
A few perfectly dried anemones make a charming bedroom arrangement.

PRESERVING IN SILICA

1 Preparing the box Line a large airtight tin or box with 3-5cm (1¼in) of desiccating agent. If your flowers have very heavy heads, put a piece of chicken wire on top of the crystals to give support to the bloom.

2 Placing the flowers Cut off the stems to about 5cm (2in) and lay the blooms carefully on the crystals. Sieve over a layer of desiccant, making sure that it gets in between the petals – use a fine paintbrush to do this if necessary.

3 Cover and seal The flowers should be covered to a depth of at least 2.5cm (1in). If your container is deep, add another layer of flowers and preservative. Then seal the box and leave in a warm place.

4 Test for readiness Take out one flower – you can get it out of the crystals on a slotted spoon. If the petals feel papery it is ready. Don't overdry or the flowers will become brittle. Flowers treated in this way should be kept and displayed in a warm dry place, or they will become limp.

All desiccants can be re-used time after time. Simply sieve out any old plant material and dry out the desiccant in a slow oven, then store in an airtight container.

SOME POPULAR PLANTS FOR DRYING

Common name	Latin name	What to dry	Method
Anemone	*Anemone*	Flowers	Dessicant
Beech	*Fagus sylvatica*	Leaves, branches	Glycerine or pressing
Bells of Ireland	*Moluccella laevis*	Flowers	Glycerine
Camellia	*Camellia*	Flowers	Desiccant
Chinese lantern	*Physalis alkekenji*	Flowers	Air dry
Cornflower	*Centaurea cyanus*	Flowers, seedheads	Air dry
Echinops	*Echninops ritro*	Seedheads	Air dry
Eucalyptus	*Eucalyptus*	Leaves	Glycerine or air dry
Strawflowers	*Helichrysum*	Flowers	Air dry
Holly	*Ilex*	Leaves	Air dry
Honesty	*Lunaria annua*	Seedheads	Air dry
Hops	*Humulus lupulus*	Flowers	Air dry
Hydrangea	*Hydrangea*	Flowers	Air dry
Ivy	*Hedera helix*	Leaves	Glycerine
Larkspur	*Delphinium consolida*	Seedheads	Air dry
Love-in-a-mist	*Nigella damascena*	Flowers, seedheads	Air dry
Peony	*Paeonia*	Flowers; leaves	Desiccant; glycerine
Pampas	*Cortaderia selloana*	Flowers, seedheads	Air dry
Pansy	*Viola*	Flowers	Desiccant
Poppy	*Papaver*	Seedheads	Air dry
Primrose	*Primula*	Flowers	Dessicant
Oak	*Quercus*	Leaves, branches	Glycerine or pressing
Oats	*Avena sativa*	Seedheads	Air dry
Ornamental onion	*Allium*	Seedheads	Air dry
Rose	*Rosa*	Flowers	Air dry or desiccant
Sea lavender	*Limonium tataricum*	Flowers	Air dry
Statice	*Limonium sinuatum*	Flowers	Air dry
Sunray	*Rhodanthe*	Flowers	Air dry
Teasel	*Dipsacus*	Seedheads	Air dry
Yarrow	*Achillea*	Flowers	Air dry

Dried flower ring

There's nothing nicer than dried flowers to brighten-up your home during the winter months with memories of summer. Here, a pretty flower ring has been used to decorate a rather dark fireplace that has also been filled to overflowing with scented cones.

This particular ring is easy to make since it uses only three types of flowers and grimmia moss. The ring base can be bought from a florist and can be re-used when you tire of the first display. This wreath will also look good displayed on your door at Christmas.

▼ *Winter welcome*
Make an unused fireplace into an attractive focal point by decorating it with pine cones and a winter wreath. Caught in the sunshine the faded colours spring to life in front of the classic cast iron fireplace.

MAKING THE RING

Materials

Florist's foam ring, for dried flowers
Florist's wire and scissors

Bunch of grimmia moss
8 large, dried hydrangea heads
6 large heads of dried yarrow or lady's mantle
30 dried rose buds

This lovely dried flower ring is quick and easy to make. Based on a foam ring and using moss as backing you will only need three types of dried flowers.

1 Attaching a loop Wire up the foam ring by attaching a loop or hook at the back to make the fixing easier later.

2 Wiring the flowers The hydrangea and yarrow heads have fairly tough dried stems, but should they break off the flower heads can still be used by adding wire stems. Simply bend a 10 cm (4 in) length of florist's wire in half, then positioning the bent end over the flower head, twist both wires together to form a new stem.

3 Starting off The moss is attached to the ring first, in fairly large clumps to give good cover. It's held in place on the ring with wire pins. Make your pins by bending 10cm (4in) lengths of florist's wire in half. Then attach the moss, by pushing the pins through the moss into the foam. Build up seven large clumps of moss randomly over the ring. Overall, the moss fills about a third of the ring.

4 Adding yarrow heads The yarrow heads are added next and are simply pushed into the ring. Try to arrange the six large yellow heads at fairly equal intervals around the ring, working the design around the moss. If you are unable to obtain yarrow you could use lady's mantle as an alternative.
   Stand back to check the effect, and alter the arrangement.

5 Inserting the hydrangea heads The hydrangea heads add a bright touch to the ring, so should be added with care. They are simply pushed into the foam. Here, eight hydrangea heads have been positioned in fairly central areas so that they fill in all the large gaps. Once you have added them all stand back to check the effect. At this stage the wreath should be completely covered. It is a good idea to choose your coloured hydrangea heads in a shade to match your room scheme.

6 Adding the roses The dried roses add the final touch and have been used to give impact and colour. Here, six bunches of roses have been added at random over the ring. Push them individually into the foam moving the existing material to one side. This makes a tight arrangement.

7 Finishing off When complete stand back to check the effect and add more moss to fill any gaps and completely disguise the ring.

Dried flower wreaths

Wreaths and garlands are traditional wall and door decorations, usually associated with Christmas. But if you use dried flowers, bought at a florist's or dried at home, you can have wreaths all the year round.

Dried flower wreaths make delightful informal displays, perfectly at home in all styles of settings. They can be used to brighten a dark corner, to decorate mirrors, mantelpieces and dressers. Hung on ribbons in toning or matching colours, wreaths can make attractive substitutes for pictures in sitting rooms and bedrooms, whether placed alone or in groups of small garlands in complementary colours. A wreath makes an excellent focal point for a dinner table, especially if you

choose colours to complement the food of your china. Finally, if your front door is sheltered in a porch, hang a dried flower wreath on it as a symbol of peace and friendship.

Although it can evoke the glories of summer gardens in full bloom, a dried flower wreath should never be treated like some poor relation of its fresh equivalent. Dried flowers have their own particular charms, notably the delicate, crispy textures and warm, muted colours. Unless you go for dyed ones, the subtle colours of dried flowers always complement one another, so your wreath's colour scheme can be easily designed to fit your existing decor, or whatever preserved plant material is available.

▲ Perfectly preserved
The combination of dried flowers, seeds and ears of wheat give this garland a real summery feel. Most of these flowers have kept their natural colours but to add a touch of brightness yarrow has been dyed a deep russet and used sparingly.

For a strong, assertive effect, try a combination of yellows, golds and purples, or glowing reds and russets. A combination of palest yellows, golds and silvers can suggest spring; yellows, oranges and russets will suggest autumn. A Christmas wreath made from lichens, fir cones and white flowers would make a lovely wintry alternative to the traditional bright reds and glossy greens of holly and ivy.

A summery wreath all year round

Using only dried flowers and foliage that are readily available from florists, you can make an attractive country wreath to adorn your house – it would look equally decorative in the hall, kitchen, bedroom or living room.

Materials

Globe thistles, yarrow, strawflowers, wheat, honesty, poppy heads, delphiniums, sea lavender, helichrysum and chinese puzzle are the ingredients of the wreath.

Apart from the flowers, you will also need a medium-size **wire wreath frame**, a bag of **sphagnum moss**, **scissors**, a **craft knife**, **reel wire**, medium **stub wire** bent into hairpin shapes, and a reel of **wreath wrap**.

MAKING THE WREATH

1 Preparing the base Break up the moss and remove any twigs and dead matter. Attach one end of the reel wire to the frame. Tightly bind clumps of moss to the frame with reel wire until the whole ring is covered with a thick layer of moss.

2 Wrapping the wreath Turn the garland over, and working from the back, bind the whole ring with wreath wrap. Overlap the tape slightly as you work, and secure each turn with a stub wire pin.

3 Covering with foliage Wire the wheat or other grassy foliage into clumps, then bind the clumps on to the frame with reel wire. Continue until the frame is covered with a thick layer of foliage.

4 Wiring bunches Holding the stem ends together, and starting 5cm (2in) up, bend a medium stub wire behind the stems. Wind the long end of the wire round the stems down to the bottom of the bunch, and leave the ends extended to insert into the frame.

honesty

wheat

wreath frame
and moss

scissors
and craft
knife

delphiniums

globe thistles

stub
wire

strawflowers

helichrysum

chinese
puzzle

reel
wire

yarrow

poppy heads

sea lavender

wreath wrap

5 **Adding the flowers** To make sure the colour in the arrangement is well balanced, start by inserting small bunches of flowers, wired individually, round the wreath. Wire the flowers close to their heads or they will droop or snap off. Keep moving the garland round to view it from the different angles.

6 **Completing the wreath** Finish off by tucking in the honesty, chinese puzzle and statice. The gypsophila, can be wired together in small clumps. Aim for a wild and slightly unruly effect.

25

Infinite possibilities

Garlands are extremely versatile; they can be frivolous, festive or formal, as the occasion demands. Working on bases of wire, vine, larch or straw you can use a dried or preserved flowers and foliage, adding fruits or gourds or pine cones for extra interest and texture.

▼ Seasonal colour
The charm of a fresh wreath of glossy evergreen leaves can be enhanced as the season allows with fresh or dried Chinese lanterns, or, for Christmas, with berries and pine cones.

▲ From garden and the hedgerow
A rustic wreath that owes little if anything to the florist's art, and proves that you can successfully dry all sorts of garden and field plants. The wire base is covered with hedgerow grasses and leaves, and then the dried flowers are dotted about, their muted colours blending easily.

◄ Dye bright
You could transform a dark corner or gloomy hall with this vibrant garland. Among the ingredients of the wreath are statice, mimosa, strawflowers, grasses, nigella, yarrow and monkshood.

Drycleaning
If your garland becomes dusty over the months, use your hairdryer, set at a low heat, to gently blow the dirt away.

Wreaths made of dried flowers, seeds, twigs and grasses are as versatile as they are varied. Use them in place of pictures, hang them on doors or place them on shelves or tabletops, wherever the room lacks focus. Make them from a single type of flower or from a mixture of favourites to create a unique decoration all your own. Let the room or proposed position of the wreath dictate its design. If it's in a dominant position, such as over a mantelpiece, then limit the varieties or colours of flowers used, as this will create a dramatic effect. Add dried grasses, ears of wheat and plants like poppy heads and honesty for a soft effect.

◄ Sweetly scented
Dried lavender not only offers subtle blue/mauve hocs but natural fragrance. Tie bunches with richly-coloured wire-edged ribbon to bring a sumptuous, period element to a simple country wreath.

▼ Scented sensation
A dark wreath made of twisted twigs is crowned with a profusion of dried damask roses and stems of lavender for a stunning effect which dominates the mantelpiece. The roses are the focus of the arrangement, while the lavender provides a contrast in colour and softens the shape.

▲ **Hearts and flowers** Dried flowers of all colours and lengths can be transformed into beautiful garlands. Here, the circular garland uses a mixture of short-stemmed flowers, while the lavender heart cleverly uses its long stems to form the distinctive shape.

▼ **Door delight** A natural, unrestrained look has been carefully cultivated in this pretty door garland. Pale wheat and glossy, evergreen leaves combine with field flower colours of yellow, orange and red for a delightfully simple effect. The wide ribbon bow adds visual impact and lift.

▲ **Ribbons and bows** An unusual and rather delicate-looking wreath has been reinforced with narrow pink ribbon and finished with a large, pink bow. Only a few flowers are needed to complete the effect.

Small-scale arrangements

D elightful small arrangements in tiny containers will fill a corner with colour. They are great fun to do without costing too much, particularly if you have dried or preserved the flowers yourself (see pages 13–16 and 17–20). These three arrangements have been made in a couple of baskets and a miniature flower pot but almost any container will do. You could try using a pretty cup and saucer, a fabric covered box or small bowl.

Obviously, to make a small flower arrangement you need to use smaller flowers and leaves or the overall effect may look top heavy or unbalanced. Choose small flower heads, such as miniature roses, or break up larger composite heads into smaller pieces.

The rose basket has been designed to be viewed from the front so it should be placed with its back to the wall on a shelf or in a display cabinet. The shallower basket looks good displayed on a low table as it is best viewed from slightly above and the all-round posy is delightful from any angle.

If you know where you are going to display the arrangement, choose flowers to fit in with the existing colour scheme. Restricting the number of colours will produce a more subtle design. One or two bright colours with white makes for a bolder display.

▲ **Small and beautiful**
Any one of these lovely little displays would look delightful on a dressing table or a bathroom shelf.

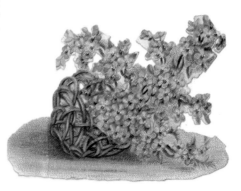

A rose basket

1 Collect together This display uses a basket with a tall handle to hold a fan shaped arrangement of dried rose buds, purple larkspur and eucalyptus leaves. You will also need oasis, florist's wire and stub wire pins, dried moss and scissors. Cut and shape the oasis to fit the basket, then cover it with moss using pins to secure.

2 Working in a line Work across the centre, positioning eucalyptus stalks and larkspur in a fan shape so that each stem of larkspur is surrounded by about five eucalyptus leaves. Make sure the shape is balanced both sides and then insert a few shorter stemmed eucalyptus and some larkspur towards the front of the display.

3 Add the rose buds Work carefully and try to fill all the spaces, using the shorter stems at the edges and building up the middle with the longer stemmed roses to give a bouquet effect. Alternate the pink and white as you work.

Shades of yellow and white

1 Collect together Mimosa, gypsophila, small chrysanthemum heads and morrison's orange form the basis of this yellow and white display, and the final touches are added by miniature roses and white helipterum. You also need a shallow basket, oasis, stub wire pins and dried moss. Cut the oasis to fit the basket.

2 Build up the shape Cover the oasis with moss, securing it with stub wire pins. Break off small sprigs of morrison's orange and insert them at intervals over the surface, taller stems at the centre and shorter stems at the edge. Add sprigs of gypsophila and mimosa in between, continuing to build up a rounded effect.

3 To finish Carefully insert the white helipterum and the miniature yellow roses at intervals making sure these larger flowers are spaced well and do not overwhelm the smaller ones. Check the arrangement from all angles, tucking in small sprigs round the edge and filling any gaps. Finally, wire a small posy of roses and chrysanthemum heads to the handle.

A posy in a pot

1 **To start** The posy uses a ball of oasis which has been glued into a small terracotta pot as a base. In addition you will need glue, dried moss, stub wire pins, miniature red roses, purple statice and bachelor's buttons, scissors and some velvet ribbon. Run a line of glue around the pot and glue the oasis ball into the pot.

2 **Add the roses** Cut the stems to about 2.5cm (1in) and work round the edge of the pot, inserting rose buds alternated with purple statice and bachelor's buttons. Continue to cover the ball, trying to avoid inserting the flowers in rows, aiming for a more random effect.

3 **To complete** Finally, place a rose bud in the centre at the top. Turn the arrangement round making sure there are no spaces left, inserting flower heads as appropriate. Then add the finishing touch of a velvet bow tied just above the edge of the pot.

Autumn harvest displays

▲ Walnuts and roses
An unusual walnut ring provides the perfect backdrop for the muted shades of a pair of dried rose bushes in terracotta pots.

The moment cut flowers start to become scarce and expensive, it's time to turn your artistic skills to creating more unusual displays with longer-lasting materials. Dried flowers are the obvious choice, but cereal grasses bunched into sheaves have enormous potential, while seed pods and nuts can look stunning as well.

Geometrically shaped displays lend themselves to this alternative dried material and generally have the great advantage of using far less material than a random display, so costs are kept to a minimum. The secret of making them successfully is to concentrate on their basic structure. Wreaths, rings, cones, pyramids and spheres made from hard foam are perfect for holding the dried or wired stems in place and can be ordered from good florists.

To give your displays a truly authentic harvest look, only select dried flowers pods, grasses and foliage in natural faded shades. More colourful, tinted, material inevitably looks harsh and false. Containers should also have the same genuinely rustic appearance so use terracotta pots in preference to plastic ones and, if possible, use older pots that have a weather-beaten patina, rather than brand new ones.

Choosing where and how to display arrangements can be just as creative as making them. Try grouping several together for real impact or make up an identical pair to stand either side of a window or fireplace. Topiary trees, such as the chestnut cone arrangment on pages 34–35, really look best displayed in this way. Another idea is to make up two or three similar arrangements but in different sizes to creat an interesting group. Whichever design you finally decide to make, check out where it will be displayed before you start to make it. The location should always dictate its size and colour scheme.

MAKING A WALNUT RING

Materials
Sphagnum moss ring wrapped in **fine wire**
Walnuts and **needle**
Stiff wire and **quick-drying glue**
Florist's wire

▲ Last roses of summer
Keep your last roses throughout autumn and winter. A dried rose arrangement is easy to make. Glue a florist's foam ball into the top of a terracotta pot, ensuring the ball rises above the rim. Cover with moss, held in place with wire pins, then add dried roses at intervals (see page 32).

1 Making a hole Use a needle to make a hole in the eye of the walnut. Dip one end of florist's wire in glue, and insert into hole. Clip wire to 4cm (1½in) long and bend end into a hook. Wire all walnuts in same way.

SWEET CHESTNUT TREE

Materials
Florist's mastic
Terracotta flower pot
Florist's prong
Florist's foam block for dried flowers
Wooden dowel
Florist's foam cone for dried flowers
Fine wire and **dried sphagnum moss**
Stiff wire with a **small nail** or **skewer**
Fresh sweet chestnuts or **conkers** from a horse chestnut tree

1 Preparing the foundation Make a cross of mastic in the base of your chosen terracotta flower pot. Fix the florist's prong to the centre of the cross. When dry give the prong a strong tug to make sure that it is firmly attached. Roughly trim the florist's foam block with a knife so that it will completely fill the pot. Push it well down into the base, impaling it securely on the prong. Using a sharp knife, cut the top surface of the foam block flush with the rim of the pot.

2 Adding the cone Push the wooden dowel well into the base, leaving enough exposed to insert a half of the way into the cone. Impale the cone centrally on the dowel.

3 Attaching the moss Cut the wire into short lengths and bend into hairpin shapes. Use them to fix the moss on to the cone, until it is evenly covered.

4 Wiring the chestnuts Using a sharp nail or skewer, make a small hole in the blunt end of each chestnut. Dip the end of a stiff wire, 4cm (1½in) long, in quick-drying glue, then insert in the hole, pushing well in. Continue until all the chestnuts are wired. Allow to dry.

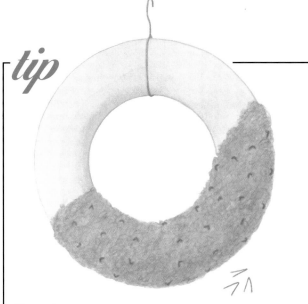

2 Attaching walnuts Fasten a wired-up walnut securely to the moss ring by inserting the wire into the ring as far as it will go. Working out from this point, start building up a walnut cover.

3 Finishing off Attach the remaining walnuts as close together as possible until the sides and front surface are fully covered.

Ring the changes

If you can't get a moss ring, use a florist's foam ring for dried flowers and sphagnum moss. Bend fine wire into hairpin shapes, and use them to hold the moss evenly all over the ring. Attach the walnuts using the same method as before, except that you will not need a hook at the end of the wire.

5 Attaching the chestnuts Starting at the base, work up the tree, inserting chestnuts fairly close together. Turn the tree as you go, to ensure even coverage. Finish with a single chestnut on top.

▶ Natural choice
This conical 'nut tree' is comprised of dried sphagnum moss studded with a spiral of sweet chestnuts. Polished conkers would also work well, as long as there is no risk of children eating the nuts.

MAKING A WHEATSHEAF

Neatly bundled sheaves of wheat instantly conjure up pictures of the countryside at harvest time. Make these miniature ones to decorate your country kitchen and remind you of those sunny days of summer.

Divide a large bunch of sheaf wheat, barley or ornamental grass into four smaller bunches. Bunch one cluster tightly and tie with string just below the ears.

Distribute the stems of the second bunch around the first, with the seed heads slightly lower, and tie securely again just below the ears.

Repeat with the third and fourth bunches, tying them tightly just below the seed heads, causing the stems to splay out. Trim the stalks evenly at the base. Finish by tying a decorative plait of raffia, twine or dried grass round the sheaf.

For a smaller wheatsheaf, work as before but with fewer stems. Once tied, the stems can be twisted with care for a more elaborate effect.

▼ Harvest bounty
A trio of old-fashioned sheaves, two of wheat and one of reed canary grass, decorate the scrubbed pine dresser in this country kitchen.

Ageing a flower pot
To remove the pristine newness from a terracotta flower pot, leave it outdoors for several months in damp shade, or for a faster effect you can paint the pot with yoghurt to encourage moss to grow. For an instant patina, rub white or pastel-coloured chalk unevenly into the surface, which will give the pot a salted effect.

Floral frame

This pretty pinboard would cost a fortune to buy from the shops, but can be made for next to nothing at home using a plain board, florists' foam, string and dried flowers. In fact you could decorate a framed picture or a mirror in exactly the same way.

The foam base is covered by wrapping it up in string, before it is stuck around the board. The flower heads and seed pods are then pressed into place to make the arrangement. Dried moss can be substituted for the string if you wish

and other items like shells, cinnamon sticks and pine cones can be wired up and added for an interesting three dimensional effect.

Use commercially available dried flowers or dry your own favourites from the garden (see pages 13–16). Some flowers such as rose buds and heathers can be enjoyed as fresh flowers first then hung to dry. While others, like the nigella seed heads, grasses and helichrysum used on this frame, are best picked fresh and hung to dry in small bunches in a

warm, well-ventilated room or cupboard.

Once you have decorated the frame remember to keep it looking good by occasionally replacing any flowers that have been knocked or damaged with others of a similar colour and shape.

▼ *Floral messages*
Frame your messages and favourite pictures in a deep floral surround. The warm colours of the dried flowers and twine blend well against the natural cork surface.

MAKING THE PINBOARD

Materials

Square cork pinboard 60cm (24in) square
Cardboard 60cm (24in) square
Dried flower and grasses with strong, rigid stems, about 6 bunches
Sharp craft scissors
PVA adhesive
Paint brush for applying adhesive
Florist's foam for dried flowers 2 blocks 23 x 11 x 8cm (9 x 4½ x 3¼in)
Cutting board, craft knife and **carving knife**
Soft natural jute garden twine 1 reel
Elastic 1.3 x 3m (2 x 3⅜in)
Drawing pins 24

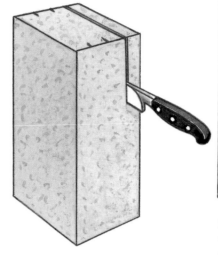

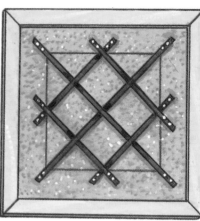

2 Cutting the florist's foam
Working on a cutting board, use a carving knife to slice each foam block into four equal 2cm (¾in) thick slices. Work from the top of the block downwards. Brush off excess dust.

3 Making the base Using PVA adhesive, stick the florist's foam to the card template, trimming the foam to fit. Leave to stick firmly.

6 Adding more elastic strips Cut the remaining elastic into four pieces. Working from the halfway point and slipping the elastic under the first diagonal, pin a piece of elastic across the two corners. Pin the last two lengths of elastic across the remaining two corners, laying them over the elastic. Secure ends with pins.

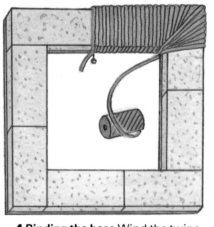

7 Sticking the base on Coat the underside of the card and pinboard with PVA adhesive and press the card firmly in place on the pinboard over elastic. Leave to dry.

1 Measuring the base Make a base from cardboard. Measure the inner frame and draw a square the size of this inner frame. Mark an 8cm (3¼in) border all round the card. Cut out the centre and discard. Fit the card inside the pinboard and mark the inner square on to the pinboard.

4 Binding the base Wind the twine around the foam-covered card. Pin the twine end in to the card and wind evenly, laying strands side-by-side. When the end has been wound over, remove the pin. Do not pull too hard. To finish, tuck the other end under the strands on the card side and stick in place.

5 Adding elastic Cut two strips of elastic 55cm (21½in) long. Pin one strip outside the marked square with drawing pins, at one corner and stretch it, diagonally across the board, to pin it to the opposite corner. Pin the second length across the border between the remaining two corners.

8 Adding flowers Trim flower and grass stems to about 2.5cm (1in) from the heads, cutting the ends at an angle. Push some of these gently but firmly into the florist's foam through the twine to form small groups. Leave some areas of twine exposed between groups of flowers.

Pot pourri

Pot pourri is a fragrant mixture of dried flower petals, aromatic herbs, seeds, spices and essential oils, which together act as an attractive natural air freshener. It is easy to make with sweetly scented flowers and foliage from your own garden, with ready-dried material from shops, or by using a combination of both of these.

The words 'pot pourri' are French for 'rotten pot', which is a reference to the ancient method of making pot pourri with fermented or rotting material, rather than dried petals and leaves.

The modern, dry method of making pot pourri is a much more pleasant procedure, with far better decorative results – the petals and leaves keeping their attractive shapes and colours. There are flowers for drying all year round. You can even preserve the scents and colours of different times of year by saving seasonal petals and florets for use in a pot pourri – for example, chrysanthemum petals and cloves evoke the rich smells and colours of autumn.

▼ **Fragrant decorations**
Pot pourri gives year-round floral delights whether displayed in pots and shallow containers or sewn into lace-edged sachets for gifts to scent drawers and wardrobes.

Below, from top to bottom:
rosebuds
hibiscus
lavender

cinnamon stick

pestle and mortar

essential oil

cloves

dried lemon peel

scented geranium leaf

Making your own

Although chemists, department stores and cosmetic companies sell pot pourri in many varieties, either ready mixed or as separate flowers and leaves, you'll miss the experience, the satisfaction and pleasure of creating your own. There are many recipes for pot pourri, but the ingredients usually fall into four main categories: flowers for scent or colour; aromatic leaves and herbs, which also add bulk; spices and citrus peel to sharpen the pot pourri's floral scent; fixatives to preserve the blend.

Once you are familiar with these basics, you can vary a recipe by adding essential oils to intensify a favourite scent or by introducing seedheads, bark, small fir cones or wood shavings for visual interest.

Materials

Flowers, leaves and herbs Make sure that all plant material is thoroughly dry before making up the pot pourri.

Spices Cinnamon, nutmeg, mace, cloves and allspice are traditional pot pourri spices, but anise, cardamom, root ginger, coriander and vanilla pods are sometimes used in exotic mixes. Freshly ground or grated spices have a stronger, clearer aroma than ones bought as powders. Cinnamon sticks, allspice and juniper berries are sometimes used whole, for textural interest.

Dried citrus peel Traditionally, oranges and lemons are used to add a refreshingly sharp contrast to floral scents, but limes, grapefruit or satsumas are also fine. Use thin-skinned fruit, or use a sharp knife or potato peeler to remove the skin with a minimum of pith attached. Flatten the peel out before drying it.

Fixatives These are used to absorb, blend and preserve the scent of dried flowers, herbs, spices and oils. Musk, ambergris and civet are traditional fixatives, but today gum benzoin, in resinous form, or powdered dried orris root are used. Gum benzoin has a vanilla-like fragrance, while orris has a faint violet scent. Both are sold by herbalists and some chemists.

Essential oils Rose, lavender, lily-of-the-valley, rose geranium, sandalwood, lemon verbena, almond, gardenia, cedarwood, eucalyptus and citronella oils are sold at many chemists and body-care shops. Use them sparingly to enhance pot pourri.

◀ Pot pourri ingredients
Spices, peel, oils, leaves and flowers are the basis for a scented mixture. Use a pestle and mortar to break up spices and release their aroma.

Making pot pourri

Try to pick all flowers, buds, leaves and herbs on a dry morning, after the dew has dried but before the sun's heat has evaporated any volatile oils, the source of plants' scent. Any plants that have been picked wet from the rain or dew are liable to rot rather than dry.

Flowers are most fragrant when fully open, and herbs are most aromatic when starting to flower.

Dry the material as soon as possible after picking, and place each type of flower and leaf on separate areas of kitchen paper, since drying times vary.

Drying

Whole stems You can air-dry small flowers by hanging the stems upside down in bunches in a dry, dark, well-ventilated spot, such as an attic (see page 15). Once the petals are papery and crisp, carefully snip the flower heads from the stems.

Small flowers Snip small fresh flowers where they join the stems and dry in a single layer on a sheet of kitchen paper, placed on a wire mesh screen or baking rack so that the air can circulate around them. Place in an airing cupboard, on top of a night-storage heater, or other warm,

dry, dark spot, for about a week, turning them over once or twice.

Large flowers Carefully remove the petals and dry them in a single layer in the same way as for small flowers.

Leaves These can be air-dried on their stems, as above, then stripped when dry. Alternatively, strip the fresh leaves from their stems, tearing larger leaves into pieces, then dry on kitchen paper.

Citrus peel Before use, thinly pared citrus rind should be spread on a sheet of paper and kept in a warm, dry place, such as an airing cupboard, for two or three days.

What to pick

For fragrance
Provence roses, damask roses, lavender, wallflower, chamomile, verbena, tansy, sweet woodruff, hyacinth, heliotrope, narcissus, pinks, tobacco plant, cotton lavender, sweet violet, lilac, sweet pea, mock orange, freesia, mimosa, lime blossom, mignonette, jasmine, honeysuckle.

For colour
Florist's roses, unopened rosebuds, zinnia, clematis, hydrangea, golden rod, larkspur, calendula, delphinium, peony, helipterum, cockscomb, marigold, pansy, mallow, nasturtium, campion, borage, globe amaranth, heather, yarrow, statice, buttercup, helichrysum, hibiscus.

For bulk and aroma
Lemon verbena, rosemary, scented geranium, lemon balm, lemon thyme, artemisia, sweet basil, sweet marjoram, costmary, bay, bergamot, myrtle, tarragon, dill, sage, various mints.

▲ *Instant pot pourri*
Make pot pourri quickly with stalks of lavender that have dried, upside down for a week or two. Crumble the heads between your fingers and display dried purple petals in a bowl.

tip

Reviving pot pourri
When a pot pourri's scent begins to fade after a couple of weeks, the mixture can be refreshed by adding a few drops of essential flower oil.

Choosing containers

Perforated china dishes or decorated china balls are traditional pot pourri containers, but to enjoy the fragrant mixture you don't need to possess such exclusive items. A pot pourri container can be any shape and made of any material. If the decorative impact is as important as the scent, use an open bowl to show off the colours of the petals. To fill a large bowl you don't need a vast quantity. Pre-pack the container with cotton wool or crumpled tissue paper, covering the top with a layer of your mixture. However, the perfume of an uncovered pot pourri fades quickly and will need reviving from time to time.

A traditional recipe

1 cup each dried rose petals and lavender
½ cup each dried rosebuds, lemon verbena leaves and scented geranium leaves
1 strip dried lemon peel
1 tsp allspice berries
1½ tsp cloves
1 cinnamon stick
2 tsp dried orris root powder
2 drops rose oil

1 The flowers Mix the dried petals, buds, lavender and leaves in a large bowl. Using scissors, cut the lemon peel into pieces and add.

2 The spices Using a pestle and mortar, crush the allspice berries and cloves. Break the cinammon stick into small pieces. Mix all the spices into the other ingredients.

3 Adding the fixative Sprinkle the orris root powder over the ingredients and mix thoroughly. Add the rose oil, and mix again.

4 Prepare for storage Place the mixture in a lidded jar and store for four weeks, shaking or gently stirring the mixture every few days so that all the scents are absorbed.

▶ **Displaying pot pourri**
These perforated containers allow the perfume to permeate gently through the room.

A winter arrangement

The beauty of informal dried flower displays is that you can put a variety of flowers together to add a splash of colour to any room. Dried flowers, seed heads, foliage and grasses come in a huge range of natural and dyed tones, and remain attractive for months on end. They are sold all year round, but are traditionally used during the winter, when fresh flowers are in short supply.

This particular display is based on rich autumnal tones, with no formal structure or focal point. For impact, it depends on a tapestry-like effect, with short-stemmed blooms hiding the stems of the taller flowers behind. On a tight budget, make a scaled-down version rather than a large, but sparse one. Try mixing contrasting forms like the typical, floral shape of roses, the solid globes of carthamus or love-in-a-mist, the poker-like spikes of love-lies-bleeding and the graceful, arching sprays of oats.

Most flowers are best grouped in small bunches, which makes building up a dense display quicker and easier than inserting individual stems. Use the dried rose and carthamus leaves to add bulk and contrast.

Any opaque container is suitable,

▲ Winter warmer
This informal arrangement uses rich autumnal colours – reds, oranges, greens and golds – which will add a touch of warmth to your home throughout the winter months.

but the rectangular terracotta garden pot shown, with its fruit and foliage swags, emphasizes a natural theme. An oval wicker basket would be just as charming, and you could add a designer touch by lightly spraying it with aerosol spray paint to tone in with the flowers.

Materials

Green love-lies-bleeding (*Amaranthus*) 1 bunch
Red love-lies-bleeding (*Amaranthus*) 1 bunch
Safflower (*Carthamus*) 1 bunch
Love-in-a-mist seed pods (*Nigella*) 1 bunch
Hydrangea flower heads 2-3
Crimson-dyed glixia 1 bunch
Red roses 2 bunches
Oats 1 bunch
1 rectangular or oval container
1 florist's dried flower foam block
1 florist's prong
florist's mastic
medium-sized stub wires

ARRANGING THE DISPLAY

1 Defining the shape Place florist's mastic into the base and press a prong on to it. Cut a foam block to fit and impale it on to the prong. Using small bunches and single stems of *Amaranthus*, define the display's height and width: 1½ times the container's height, and slightly wider than the rim.

2 Filling in Cut the *Carthamus* and *Nigella* stems 2.5-5cm (1-2in) shorter than the *Amaranthus*, and group into single-type clusters, stripping the lowest *Carthamus* leaves. Insert the clusters at random to begin building up a dome shape.

3 Building density Cut the large hydrangea flower heads into four sections. Loop a stub wire through each section to form a stem, and insert at random, at the same height as the *Carthamus*. View from different angles as you work to ensure you have an even effect.

4 Adding red Group the glixia into bunches, since these are too small to be used singly. Cut the stems as for the *Carthamus*, and insert at random. Cut the rose stems to come half way between the general mass and *Amaranthus*, and remove the lowest leaves. Insert singly, in pairs and in small groups, filling in any large gaps as you do so.

5 Finishing off Cut the oat stems at the same height as the roses, and group into bunches. The oats are the palest and most eye-catching element, and need careful, even positioning. Stand back to check the arrangement and reposition any oats which look out of place.

Oats

Love-in-a-mist

Hydrangea flower heads

Red roses

Green love-lies bleeding

Crimson-dyed glixia

Safflower

Red love-lies bleeding

Dried flower swags

▲ A sumptuous swag
Laden with fragrant cinnamon, gilded cones, plump artificial fruits, nuts and brilliant dried red roses; this opulent swag transform a humble fireplace into a festive focal point.

▲ A nutty collection
Nuts can be glued on to lengths of stout wire, then wired together in bunches and bound on to swags.

Richly coloured swags of dried flowers and foliage make delightful decorations for a really special occasion. Long lasting, they add a permanent styling detail to a kitchen or formal hallway – simply renew them every autumn, when the materials are plentiful. Masses of dried flowers, treated foliage, grasses, fruit and nuts can look wonderful hanging in festoons. Dried swags are particularly suitable for harvest festival or Christmas – or any time when fresh flowers are difficult to obtain. Arrange a single swag across a chimney breast or over a doorway. For a more elaborate display, loop a series of swags along the front of a table, or at the top of a dresser. Twine garlands of dried flowers between the bannisters up a stairway, or around pillars and posts in the centre of a marquee.

Materials

A piece of chicken wire, the length of the finished swag and at least 20cm (8in) wide, to hold moss.

Stub wires are used to attach the flower heads to the base.

Flexible wire is used to bind plant material in place. Plastic-coated green garden wire is particularly useful for binding foliage.

Hairpins can also be used to hold plant material in place.

Pliers and wire cutters for bending and cutting wire.

Gardening gloves or **heavy rubber gloves** should be worn when wiring the swag; they will help to prevent your hands being scratched by any sharp materials.

The base

For the best results, choose a natural-looking base, which will tone in with the dried flowers. Dry sphagnum moss provides an ideal base for a dried swag and is available from garden centres. In this chapter, the moss has been rolled into a sausage-shape and then wrapped in chicken wire, which gives some flexibility to the swag. The moss-filled wire can be rolled or flattened and shaped to build up a formal swag.

You could also use loosely-plaited sisal or a length of decorative cord. These bases make more flexible swags for twining and twisting around uprights, or looping across tables or dressers.

Plant materials

For short-term displays, you can combine dried flowers with ever-green foliage, which will hold its colour, leaves or needles for a week or so – even in centrally heated rooms. But for a more permanent display, use only dried materials.

Choose a colour scheme and select materials carefully to suit the occasion. The plant material must be of good quality and not crumble or shed leaves or petals easily. For easier handling, make up the swag with your own dried material, using it before it is completely dry: when finished, hang the swag in a dark, airy place to continue drying naturally.

Covering the base

Choose a plentiful material for the body of the swag, to cover and disguise the wire and moss base completely, and to create the basic shape of the swag. Fresh or glycerine-treated foliage always works well. Or use dried flowers, such as *gypsophila*, statice or sea holly which can be treated like foliage. Hang tails of foliage at each end of a single swag, or at the joints between swags.

Dried flowers These should be left on their stalks wherever possible, but trim the stalks to even lengths – about 10-15cm (4-6in) long. To make the most of scarcer dried flowers, group them together at the centre of the swag to create a focal point. Echo this centre-piece with two small arrangements; one at each end of the swag.

▲ **Well matched**
Red roses, lavender, golden leaves and green foliage perfectly enhance their background.

PLANT COMBINATIONS

Some suggested combinations of plant material are listed below.

Harvest swag
Glycerine-treated beech (*Fagus sylvatica*)
Bunches of dried woody-stemmed herbs, including bay, thyme, rosemary and lavender
Ears of wheat and barley or other dried grasses
Small apples
Dried red and green peppers, still on their stems

Christmas swag
Yew or other conifer
Variegated ivy
Holly
Gold and silver sprayed dried flower heads, such as Bells of Ireland (*Moluccella laevis*), strawflowers (*Helichrysum bracteatum*) and statice (*Limonium sinuatum*), or use white and gold dried flowers
Red ribbon bows

Special occasion swag
Box and variegated ivy
Dried flowers (baby's breath (*Gypsophila elegans*), white and pink everlastings (*Helipterum manglesii*), white and pale shades of statice (*Limonium sinuatum*, rose-buds, allium heads, lavender heads, sea holly (*Eryngium maritimum*)

Kitchen swag
Sea holly (*Eryngium maritimum*)
Dried golden yarrow (*Achillea filipendulina*) lady's mantle (*Alchemilla mollis*), strawflowers (*Helichrysum bracteatum*)
Small gourds
Sprays of rose hips

Preparation

The plant materials need to be prepared and then wired on to the moss-filled base. Firstly, foliage or background flowers are wired to cover the base, creating the body of the swag. Then individual flowers, sprigs and sprays or small bunches of flowers, bound together, are used to build up the swag. Wiring flower heads not only enables you to arrange them precisely, but also gives a secure method of fixing.

For details of how to wire dried flowers before attaching them to the swag, see page 12. Foliage can be wired in various ways, according to the type.

Small flowers can be wired in bunches for greater impact. Cut the stems 5cm (2in) long and bind them with wire. Leave trailing wires to secure to the swag.

Short sprigs of flowers can be stabbed to the swag using hairpins or lengths of wire bent in half.

Glycerine-treated **beech**, fresh sprigs of **fir**, **box** or **ivy** can simply be laid along the length of the base. Then bind the stems in place.

Holly is trickier to handle. It is easier to wire individual leaves, and attach to the swag by poking the wire stubs into the base.

Improvise wiring to suit the material you are using. For example, if you plan to use apples and round gourds, wire each fruit with two heavy stub wires. Push the wires in horizontally, at right angles to one another, then twist the two ends together to form a single stem to tie into the chicken wire. Avoid using very heavy fruit.

▲ Festive swag
A swag, made from leaves, cones and flowers has been draped across this beautifully painted fireplace for a festive touch.

▼ Dressing a dresser
Delicate pastel shades of lilac, peach, lemon, cream and various greens are combined to make this dried flower swag.

MAKING A SWAG

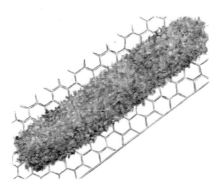

1 Trim the chicken wire to the required size: it should be the same length as the finished swag, and wide enough to form a cylinder the width of the swag plus an overlap of 7.5-10cm (3-4in). If possible, cut the wire with one finished straight edge of the chicken along the length of the swag.

2 Arrange a sausage of dry sphagnum moss along the length. Start to wrap the wire around the moss, overlapping the long edges and twisting the loose ends of the wire into the mesh to form a cylindrical base.

3 For larger swags, squash the filled mesh into the desired shape. The ends may be tapered.

4 Wire up the ends of the base, leaving wire tails or loops for hanging the swag if necessary.

5 Build up the plant material, wiring foliage in place a branch at a time along the length of the swag. Start from the tip of each branch, and work towards the base. Overlap branches along the length of the swag.

6 Add more prepared plant material to suit the design. Bend the stub wire around a hairpin and stick the hairpin into the swag, or insert the stub wire through the swag and twist the end into the mesh. Make sure all unsightly wires are buried in the body of the swag, or covered by adjacent decorations.

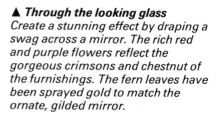

▲ Through the looking glass
Create a stunning effect by draping a swag across a mirror. The rich red and purple flowers reflect the gorgeous crimsons and chestnut of the furnishings. The fern leaves have been sprayed gold to match the ornate, gilded mirror.

Draping
Although you are working on a flat table top, you must remember that the swag will hang when finished. Hold up the swag to see how gravity will affect your work. Make sure flower heads don't turn downwards and heavy items do not droop.

Pressing flowers

Pressing is one of the best methods of preserving the natural beauty of flowers. Simply by placing freshly cut blooms between sheets of absorbent paper under pressure, the flower's moisture is absorbed, leaving a flat, and often brightly coloured bloom.

Once pressed the flowers can be used to create pictures, decorate greetings cards and gift tags, make jewellery, adorn pot lids and even furniture.

You will find there are several methods of pressing flowers and leaves all equally effective providing they are done properly. The most commonly used method is to press flowers between sheets of absorbent paper (such as blotting paper) within a large book, which has been heavily weighted by further books placed on top.

▼ Perfectly preserved
Once you get the knack of pressing flowers you can become more adventurous and even make other items for the home. These pressed flower pictures are simple to make and look good anywhere around the home.

Another method of pressing involves placing your flowers between two sheets of absorbent paper and then sliding them into the middle of a folded newspaper beneath a carpet.

But the ideal method is to use a large flower press. This is constructed with layers of plywood which can be tightened by four bolts to apply maximum even pressure.

The length of time flowers should remain under pressure, depends on the type of flower and its moisture content; basically it is a matter of trial and error. Once the moisture has been absorbed by the paper the flowers are ready for use. Two to three weeks is probably the maximum pressing time.

In the case of tiny flowers the pressing may take only a couple of days. If you leave the flowers for too long, the petals will start to discolour.

It is a good idea to experiment with flowers and foliage of different types to work out approximate pressing times for each species.

Gathering flowers

Whether you live in the town or country you will find an endless variety of flowers and foliage to choose from. Don't restrict yourself to the plants growing in your garden; search among the hedgerows, woods and meadows, and look for interesting grasses and foliage.

It is a good idea to familiarize yourself with the plants in your local area, particularly with any of the endangered species, as it is now illegal to pick any flowers which belong to this group.

Even with common varieties don't pick all the flower heads from a single plant; remember, careless gathering can lead to rarity in years to come.

When to pick

Always pick your flowers on a dry day once the dew has evaporated. Wet specimens will fade and can go mouldy when pressed. If you are out on a damp day and chance upon a particularly fine species, you could pick a couple of blooms with long stems and leave them to stand in a vase of water until the dew evaporates.

It is important to press flowers as soon as possible after they have been picked – particularly wild flowers as these have a tendency to wilt after just a few minutes.

The flowers will last longer if you place them in sealed plastic bags, taking care not to put too many in each. Alternatively, make a travelling press from blocks of wood, in which you can store the wild flowers when you are out walking.

Book pressing flowers

Materials

Flowers choose a selection to press
Books, the heavier the better, to press the flowers
Absorbent paper
Tweezers round ended ones are the best
Scissors

BOOK PRESSED FLOWERS

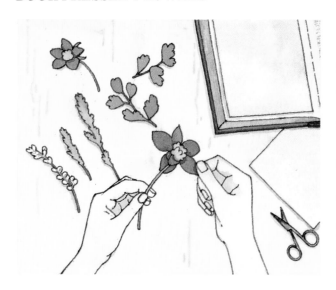

1 Preparation Take your flowers by the stalks and study them. Flat flowers need no preparation, but larger blooms such as roses need to be pressed petal by petal, and should be carefully separated before you begin.

2 Arranging the flowers Place a sheet of absorbent paper between the pages of a large, heavy book and arrange your flowers so that none are touching. Press flowers of a similar thickness.

50

Flowers for pressing

There are few flowers that cannot be successfully pressed, but simple flattish flowers such as pansies and forget-me-nots give the best results.

Large fleshy flowers, like roses, will not press well if treated in the same way as the flatish flowers; they must be taken apart and the petals pressed separately.

Other flowers, such as foxglove and delphinium work best if they are removed from their stems.

Some flowers retain their colour perfectly when pressed, others do not. Orange and yellow flowers are particularly good. Reds and pinks, however, sometimes lose their colour, but this also depends on the type of flowers. The only way to find out what will press perfectly and what won't, is to spend time experimenting with various coloured blooms.

Working with pressed flowers

It is essential to get a good supply of flowers and foliage before you start even the smallest project. When you have pressed a large quantity, store them in separate paper or greaseproof bags, labelled for easy identification.

Work in a draughtproof room so there is no danger of the featherlight blooms being disturbed and take care when moving your other materials around; the draught created by placing a piece of paper on the table can scatter flowers everywhere.

Once you have decided on your method of display – a card, a picture or even a bookmark – sketch a small plan of the basic arrangement; you can place the flowers freehand on your background, but they are frequently too delicate to move around if you change your mind.

When working with tiny flowers such as forget-me-nots use a pair of round-ended tweezers and a small paint brush to move them around.

Use a latex-based or water-based glue rather than a clear contact adhesive.

3 Pressing Place a piece of absorbent paper on top of the flowers and gently close the book. Place the book in a position where it will be undisturbed and weigh the top with further books for maximum pressure.

4 Removing the flowers When the flowers are ready for use – this can be any time from two days to a few weeks – carefully open the book and remove the specimens with tweezers, gently easing any that are stuck.

Cutting rose-buds Fleshy heads can be cut lengthways, and then pressed. Carefully slice through the centre of the flower's head with a sharp knife and press them with the cut side face down, on the absorbent paper.

Flattening blooms Primrose-like flowers have their petals joined by a small tube. For an even flower shape carefully remove the stalk and snip off the tube with scissors. Again, press the flower face down.

Pressing stems Most leaves need little preparation before pressing. However, thicker stalks will look clumsy when pressed; these can be pared down with a sharp knife.

Pressed-flower card

Hand-made greetings cards are easy-to-make and because they are home-made and give a personal touch which will make the cards a pleasure to receive.

Sunlight will damage the delicate colours of your card. Covering the bookmarks with sticky-backed translucent film helps to conserve the pressed flower arrangement.

Materials
Stiff card 20 x 30cm (8 x 12in)
Pressed flowers and **leaves**
Latex adhesive and **paint brush**
Sticky-backed plastic
Pencil and **craft knife**
Ruler

PRESSED FLOWER CARD

▲ **Bookish ideas**
Give coffee-table books a treat with their own home-made bookmarks.

▲ **Personal greeting**
Hand-made cards add an exclusive touch to your gifts.

1 Preparing the card Fold the card in two. Draw a design for your card on rough paper. Then position your flowers following your design.

2 Attaching the flowers Once you have decided on the best design glue the leaves and flowers down. Use a small quantity of clear glue, to avoid making the flowers too wet.

3 Finishing the card Rub out any pencil marks. Cover the design with sticky backed plastic.

A pressed flower picture

An object of beauty in itself, a pressed flower picture can evoke warm memories of long and hot summers past and become a lasting souvenir of a memorable holiday or even a special day out in the countryside. If the flowers themselves were given as a present, you may wish to preserve them and the picture is a perfect way to make the special gift last longer. (For instructions on how to press flowers, see pages 49–52).

Planning the picture

The first thing to consider when planning a pressed flower picture is the size of the frame you will be using in relation to the flowers' size. If you already have a selection of pressed flowers, their size, type and colour will help you to decide on the style of the finished picture.

Alternatively, your picture may be inspired by the fresh flowers growing in your garden or in nearby hedgerows, in which case select only perfect blooms, without tears or blemishes, making sure that they are not protected species, and press as described on pages 49–52.

▼ Floral reminder
This pressed posy of rock roses, larkspur and potentilla brings memories of long summer days in the garden and walks in the country.

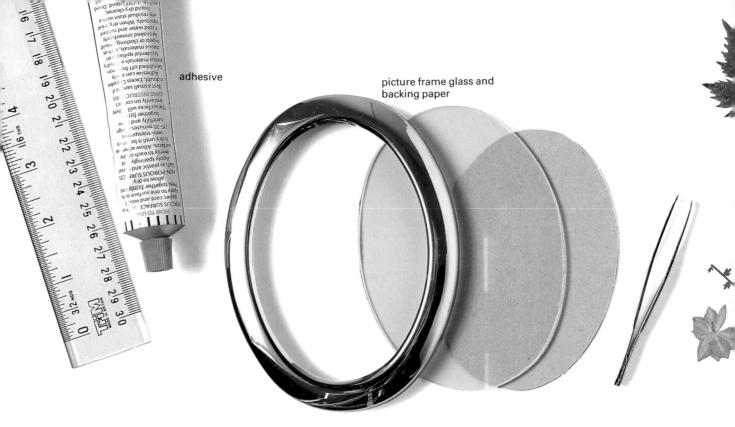

adhesive

picture frame glass and
backing paper

Choosing the background

Think carefully about the colour and texture of the background material as this will set the mood for the whole picture.

Paper There is an enormous range of papers available, most of which would make ideal backgrounds for pressed flower designs. Hand-made and marbled papers from art shops are extremely attractive and subtle enough for most pictures. Alternatively, you could use scraps of wallpaper or pale watered silk for more formal arrangements.

Fabric You can use any fabric as a backing for your picture. Cool neutral hessians, cottons and linens will create a natural country feel, while silks, velvets and brocades give your picture an opulent Victorian look. Experiment with scraps of lace and ribbon to make attractive borders and bows.

Design ideas

The design of your picture must be worked out before you start to stick the flowers down. Although you will need to experiment with flowers and foliage to establish how the shapes and colours fit together, they are often too delicate to put up with constant handling. It is a good idea to sketch out a plan on a piece of paper before you start, to use as a guide when positioning your flowers.

Colour, texture and tone are as important to a picture made with pressed flowers as they are to a painting or drawing. Just as the painter can bring a picture to life with the use of careful colour and composition, so the flower artist can create something special by being creative and using available materials to their best advantage.

Size You need to consider the size of the frame in relation to the flowers. If you have already chosen the flowers buy an appropriately sized frame; if however you have a favourite frame choose flowers which complement it.

Colour Decide on a theme or colour scheme before starting your design and try to stick to it. Obviously your choice of colours will depend to some extent on what is available, but a little discerning choice at the outset can determine the success of the finished result.

For example pale colours often produce a romantic picture while warm reds and yellows make for a mellow autumnal glow. A monochromatic arrangement has more impact than one which includes every colour of the rainbow.

Although many flower petals are generally smooth, they often have coloured veins or are flecked and speckled in a contrasting colour which can make them valuable elements in a composition. When choosing flowers watch out for the overall tones, because some blues, for example may clash with yellows. It is important to try the arrangement, before sticking the flowers down.

All pressed flowers will mellow with time, so bear this in mind when creating a bright design. Sunlight and strong illumination both affect the natural colours causing them to fade. Where possible keep your finished picture out of direct light – this should help to conserve its brilliance for many years.

Shape and texture Leaves and flowers naturally have these qualities and should be used to their best advantage in your design. Try contrasting smooth flower petals with rough textured leaves.

Foliage is enormously varied incorporating spiky feathery or rounded forms that provide a necessary contrast to the finer texture of many blooms. Other natural forms such as leaf skeletons, seeds, catkins, lichens and even shells have all been successfully introduced into dried flower pictures.

Tone Tones are light and dark areas of the picture and these can be as important to a finished work as the actual colour. Unless you specifically want a very pale or very dark overall effect it is generally a good idea to use a range of contrasting tones in a composition. Try placing dark shapes on light ones and paler colours on deeper ones. This ensures that the shape and details of the subject show up to advantage and do not merge into the colours behind them. It is helpful to have a choice of dark, light and medium coloured flowers and leaves to hand before you start to build up the picture.

tip

Treating flowers

Pressed flowers can be successfully sprayed with aerosol paint for dramatic effect. White cow parsley placed against a black background conjures up the image of falling snowflakes, while gold and silver flowers and leaves add a festive touch to any picture. Spray your flowers on a large sheet of newspaper – delicate blooms may need securing with a pin to prevent them blowing away.

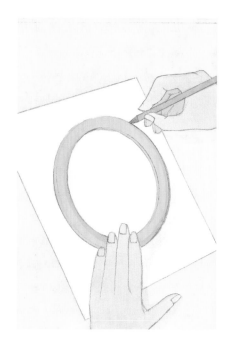

PRESSED FLOWER POSY

This beautiful posy with its wonderful shades of blue, red, white and yellow is the ideal picture for anywhere around your home; try placing it on a favourite bedside table or even in an alcove display in the lounge.

Following the plan you can make up a similar picture or use it as a guide to help you create your own original and quite different design.

Remember that size is important; many tiny blooms will make the picture look busy, larger blooms may dominate the design especially if you are using small, fine stems as a central element in the picture.

Materials
Picture frame
Background
Scissors
Latex or **water based adhesive** that dries clear
Ruler
Selection of pressed flowers (rock roses, verbena, potentilla, miniature rose, silver weed and **other foliage**
Small paintbrush
Round-ended tweezers

1 Cutting out Decide on the colour of the card for the background then cut it to the same dimensions as your picture frame. It's probably easiest to draw around the outside of the glass with a pencil to get the correct size and shape. Using a ruler measure your background lengthways and widthways to calculate the centre of the picture and mark it. This will help with the positioning of your pressed flowers.

2 Positioning foliage Arrange the background silver weed, miniature roses and verbenas on the card in a circle on the card to define the posy outline. If you are going to use different flowers it is a good idea to make a rough plan before you start. Then carefully dab a very small dot of glue on to each flower and reposition in place.

3 Completing the design Build up the picture filling in the centre of the posy with potentilla and the smaller rock roses, again checking the position of the flowers carefully before you start to glue the flowers. Finally add the larger rock roses, and carefully glue in place to complete the design.

4 Framing the work Leave the picture to dry thoroughly. It is best to leave the picture in a draught free place overnight. Then place the glass over the flowers and carefully frame the pressed flower picture.

▶ Little and large
Bold shaped leaves and
flowers in darker shades
make this placemat and
coaster a stylish duo.

▲ Gilt-edged
Smaller pictures always look good if
they are framed as a set, and these
two complementary designs are no
exception. The careful choice of
frame helps highlight the flowers.

▶ Squaring up
This pressed flower posy picture is
very similar to our step-by-step
picture on page 55, yet it looks quite
different because it has been framed
in a rectangular dark wood frame.

A pressed flower box

Arrange pressed flowers in a lasting display on the top of a small trinket box. Use this technique to decorate old wooden boxes, which can often be found at bargain prices in junk or second-hand shops; alternatively, use pressed materials to add a personal touch to a plain, new wooden box.

Whether new or old, the box will benefit from being carefully painted or stained before being decorated: it is best to use a light wash of diluted water-based paint, such as acrylic or gouache. Once dressed with the floral collage, it will make a distinctive ornament or gift.

◄ Perfect pansies
Pansies with their distinctive and varied marking are perfect for pressing.

▼ Floral trinket box
Transform a plain wooden box with a subtle wash of colour and a dainty collage of pressed flowers.

Materials

Pressed flowers and foliage are sold by specialist suppliers. To press your own, see pages 50–52.

Adhesive Use a rubber-based or spray adhesive available from craft and art supply shops.

Heat-sealed transparent film This is a clear film, with one sticky side, used to seal and protect pressed flower designs. The film stretches as it is heated, so it is ideal for covering the raised surfaces of a flower collage. It is available from craft shops, as well as specialist dried and pressed flower mail order firms.

Sponge A heat resistant sponge is needed to protect the surface of the film and collage when it is ironed. Foam rubber, about 1cm (⅜in) thick is suitable.

Paints and varnish Use an oil-based paint or stain to colour the box if desired. Protect the paint or stained surface with a few coats of oil-based varnish.

Wooden boxes Unstained, natural timber boxes are available from craft and art suppliers in a range of sizes and shapes. Alternatively decorate an old box.

Materials

Pressed flowers and foliage
Oil-based paint or stain
Rubber-based adhesive
Tweezers and toothpick
Scissors or scalpel
Protective film
Heat-resistant sponge
Iron
Oil-based varnish
Wooden box

PREPARATION

1 Paint or stain the box to the desired colour. Alternatively leave as natural timber. Check that the box lid is completely clean and free of dust.

2 Select the plant material to be used. To plan the design, trace the size of the box lid on to a piece of paper and use tweezers to gently position the foliage and flowers on to this. Take care not to damage delicate pieces.

WORKING THE COLLAGE

1 Apply a thin, even layer of glue to the area to be covered with the chosen pressed plant material.

2 Transfer the larger elements from the paper, picking them up with tweezers and carefully positioning them on to the glue.

3 Build up the collage by working on each area until satisfied with the density and shape of the arrangement. If any areas of floral material overlap apply a small amount of glue where necessary, to help hold the individual flowers or leaves in place.

tip

Sealing
If any areas look silvery after being heated, then film has not fully adhered to the surface. Reapply foam and heated iron to these areas.

4 When the picture is complete, cut transparent film to fit box lid. Carefully peel off the backing paper, avoiding static build-up by holding one corner with a slightly dampened finger. Keep backing. Lay the protective film over the top of the box, taking care not to lift or bend any of the pressed flowers or foliage on the lid.

5 Heat iron to wool setting (110°C). Put box on ironing board and cover film with backing paper, shiny side down. Place sponge on top. Press heated iron to sponge for two minutes. If work is larger than the surface of the iron, re-position iron and hold down for further two minutes. Repeat to heat the entire surface.

6 Remove sponge and backing paper and check that film has sealed. If there are any air bubbles, prick the bubble and area around it with a fine needle. Cover with backing paper and sponge and apply iron for further two minutes.

7 Trim edges of film to fit snugly on box lid. Apply heated iron to edges, as before. Varnish sides of box with a plain or coloured varnish and allow to dry.

Decorating candles

Add a special finishing touch to home-made candles by sealing delicate designs of real pressed flowers and foliage into the wax. This type of decoration is especially suitable for scented candles, as you can choose the flower to suit the fragrance.

Straight-sided, white or plain-coloured candles look prettier when decorated with pressed flowers and leaves. Flower-bedecked candles are more ornamental than useful as the pressed flower design may catch fire when the candle is burning. To prevent this happening, use very wide candles which will burn down inside, leaving the exterior design intact; alternatively, arrange the flowers near the base of the candle and let the candle burn no further than the top of the decoration. Dried flower materials can either be applied, by various methods (see page 60), to the candles once they have been made, or incorporated into the molten wax of the candle before it sets, by placing it inside the mould.

However, candles made in shaped rubber moulds or those made with crumbled herbs are not suitable for decorating.

▼ Welcome glow
Flickering flames enhance the pretty pressed flower decoration on these candles. Grouped together, they make an enchanting table display for any special occasion. They would also look super displayed as a single centrepiece on a coffee table for a party evening.

Matching the fragrance

Pressed flowers and leaves can be chosen solely for their appearance – shape, colour and texture – but it is more interesting to match the decorative design to the fragrance of the candle as well. For example, if a candle has been scented with fresh herb sprigs, use pressed sprigs of the same herb as decoration. Alternatively, if a flower-scented perfume has been used, decorate the candle with the pressed heads or petals of the matching flower.

Planning the design

Before applying the pressed flowers or herbs to the candle, plan the arrangement. Bear in mind the shape and size of the candle when deciding the position of the pressed material.

Use the pressed materials singly or grouped together to make delicate, posy-like arrangements. For instance, the sides of a square-shaped candle could be decorated with either one large flower such as a pansy, or a small arrangement of mixed flowers. When using tall, cylindrical candles it is better to twist sprigs of pressed herbs up and around the sides. On thinner candles arrange smaller leaves in a spiral pattern.

Decorating candles

The most successful way to decorate ready-made candles is to use a small amount of melted wax to seal the pressed materials in place. This method ensures a smooth professional finish to the candles.

Using melted wax

Materials

A tall, straight-sided candle
Pressed flowers, sprigs of herbs or pressed leaves of your choice
A special dipping can or similar tall, narrow, metal container
Enough melted wax of the same type as the original candle to cover the candle when it is immersed
Tweezers
Paint brush

APPLYING DECORATION

1 Plan the arrangement of the pressed material before starting.

2 Put the dipping can into a pan of water and gently melt wax; heat to a temperature of 82°C (180°F).

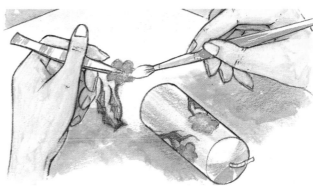

3 Using tweezers, pick up the first piece of pressed material; dab a small amount of wax on to the back of it with a paint brush. Quickly place the pressed material on to the candle and gently press so it stays in place, taking care not to tear delicate petals. Continue in this way until all the flowers and leaves are in place.

4 After the last piece has been put on, put the candle to one side to allow wax to dry completely.

5 For a smooth finish, hold the candle by its wick and dip it into a pan of molten wax. Hold it there for 10 seconds and then remove. Stand it on a flat surface so that the base will dry evenly. Repeat the dipping once more in the same way.

6 Leave the candle for at least two hours to dry completely. For a professional-looking, glossy finish, polish the candle with a soft tissue dipped in a little vegetable oil.

Alternative methods
The following methods give quick, alternative ways to apply the pressed material.

In the candle mould
Candles can be decorated as they are being made. Arrange a few dried flowers or leaves around the inside edge of the mould; add the molten wax in the usual way and leave to set. When the candle is removed from the mould the design will be set into the surface of the candle. Polish the surface to give a neat, glossy finish.

Hot water method
This involves softening the wax slightly by holding the candle by the wick and dipping it in hot water for a few seconds. Then gently roll the softened candle over some dried herb leaves or flowers and leave to dry.

Protective film
Using tweezers, pick up one flower at a time and dab a little clear glue on to the wrong side; then position on to the candle. Repeat until the design is complete. Then, allowing an extra 6mm (¼in) above the design, cover the flowers with clear protective film, takig care not to trap any air bubbles, especially around the flowers.